SPRITZ
& FIZZ

First published in 2024 by OH
An Imprint of HEADLINE PUBLISHING GROUP

2 4 6 8 10 9 7 5 3 1

Cataloguing in Publication Data is available from the British Library

Hardback ISBN 978-1-03541-914-2

Printed and bound in China

HEADLINE PUBLISHING GROUP
An Hachette UK Company
Carmelite House
50 Victoria Embankment
London EC4Y 0DZ

Publisher: Lisa Dyer
Editorial Assistant: Saneaah Muhammad
Contributing writer: Theresa Bebbington
Designer: Lucy Palmer
Production: Arlene Lestrade

www.headline.co.uk
www.hachette.co.uk

SPRITZ & FIZZ

60 SPARKLING COCKTAIL RECIPES

Illustrations by Julia Murray

Contents

Introduction

Casual get-togethers, formal parties and special celebrations – there's always a good time to pop open the bubbly! In *Spritz & Fizz*, sparkling cocktails take centre stage with twists on classics like the French 75 and Paloma Mimosa, tropical fun with the Drunken Mermaid and Pineapple Frosecco and winter wonders such as the Nordic Sunrise and Snowball.

Sparkling wines add an enjoyable fizz and subtle background flavours to a cocktail. One of the oldest cocktails, dating to the mid-1800s, is the classic champagne cocktail, in which champagne is poured over a lump of sugar soaked with a few dashes of Angostura bitters, before adding a lemon twist (for our version, see page 122). Even easier is Kir Royale, which matches crème de cassis with champagne, replacing the white wine first used in this blackcurrant-flavoured cocktail in 1904. From these easy cocktails, there are now hundreds to choose from, such as the Juniper Royale (see page 20).

Spritzes are a type of aperitif popular in Italy that combines prosecco with digestive bitters and soda water. One such drink is the Aperol Spritz (see page 78). Another is the bellini, an all-time favourite in which prosecco is mixed with peach pureé. Like the spritz, the fizz is also perfect for summertime sipping and combines sparkling water and citrus juice with a spirit.

On the following pages you will find 60 delectable recipes for every occasion and time of year. The book is divided into a section for each season – so you can enjoy cocktails with strawberries in the warm months when at their peak, with refreshing cucumber in the hot summer and with warming ginger for the colder autumn and winter months.

There are elegant sparklers for wedding events, bellinis for boozy brunches and summertime spritzes for any-day drinking. Whether you're a champagne purist, like to mix your fizz with spirits and fancy liqueurs or favour lighter soda-based tipples, there's a drink for you.

Sparkling Wines

Champagne has been the most popular of the sparkling wines for centuries, but it's facing stiff competition from others, especially with the explosion in popularity of prosecco. But what exactly is a sparkling wine, and which one should you choose?

Any wine that has a good level of carbon dioxide gas (CO_2) is a sparkling wine, and this is what creates the bubbles and gives it fizz! White and rosé wines are often used for sparkling wines, but there are also red varieties. Once you know the differences between sweet and brut and their flavour profiles, you'll soon be able to decide on a champagne, a prosecco or even a cava for your Ritz Fizz (see page 92) or Vanilla Bourbon Fizz (see page 124).

Sweet & Dry Wines

A sweet sparkling wine is usually produced by using a naturally sweet-tasting variety of grape such as moscato grapes, or by adding greater quantities of sugar to the wine. At the other end of the scale are dry wines, which are produced by allowing the yeast to feed on the sugar for longer, so there is less sugar remaining in the wine. Look for these terms on the label:

Extra Brut: with practically no sugar content, this is the driest of the sparkling wines.
Brut: these wines are dry with a hint of sweetness – they are one of the most popular types, especially in the production of champagne.
Extra Dry: confusingly, while these are considered dry wines, they are sweeter than the bruts – prosecco falls into this category.
Demi-sec: perfect choice for pairing with desserts, this is the sweetest type.

Champagne

The king of the sparkling wines, champagne was first enjoyed at the coronations of the French kings in the fifth century, and only wines produced in the Champagne region of France can be called champagne. These wineries use chardonnay along with other grape varieties to produce champagne, which needs a minimum of 15 months to several years to mature. The taste profile can be described as complex, dry and from light to full-bodied. If it's allowed to mature, its flavours have been likened to toasted bread and brioche.

Prosecco

Named after a village in Trieste, Italy, prosecco has become the rising star threatening to take on champagne. It is made with glera grapes that produce a light, refreshing, dry (or brut) sparkling wine at an affordable price. The quantity of bubbles in the bottle can vary: 'frizzante' on a label indicates a gentle fizz, while 'spumante' means there is plenty of fizz. Expect medium to high acidity with zesty, white fruit flavours. Unlike champagne, prosecco doesn't improve with age – if you have a bottle, drink it while it's still fresh.

Cava

Originating from Catalonia in Spain, cava uses the Spanish grapes macabeo, xarel-lo and parellada. These are less acidic than those used in champagne, offering more fruitiness and a fresh taste. However, also like champagne, cava has gentle effervescence and creaminess. Styles vary from sweet to very dry, filled with the fruity flavours of citrus, apple and pear.

Asti Spumante

From Piedmont, Italy, asti spumante is made from sweet moscato grapes. This light, fruity sparkling wine has a characteristic effervescence and noted grape taste, as well as flavours of peach and orange blossom.

Crémant

This sparkling French wine uses the same production process as champagne, but it's from different regions of the country so cannot be called champagne. In general, it is less acidic, as well as more fruity and less sweet, though creamy.

Sparkling Mixers

Many of the recipes in this book use a sparkling mixer along with a sparkling wine, or sometimes instead of one. Here's a rundown on the different types.

Sparkling Waters

Sparkling waters are an excellent choice if you wish to add fizziness to your drinks but not much flavour or sweetness. If you're wondering whether soda water (club soda), sparkling mineral water, tonic water and seltzer are all the same, the answer is yes, but no!

Sparkling mineral water is the only one that comes already filled with bubbles from a natural source, such as a spring or well (but some producers do boost the bubbles by adding carbon dioxide). Depending on the water's source, bottled sparkling mineral water contains different minerals, such as sodium, magnesium and calcium.

For the other varieties of sparkling water, carbon dioxide gas is the magic ingredient that is injected into water to make it sparkle. When it comes to soda water (club soda), manufacturers also add minerals that uplift the flavour profile by adding a hint of saltiness. A German original, seltzer is similar to soda water, but usually comes without the added minerals. Soda water and seltzer water can be used interchangeably as cocktail mixers in recipes, but if you need to consider salt (or sodium) content, make seltzer water your go-to option. There are also many varieties of sparkling water infused with fruit flavours, such as hibiscus, yuzu and watermelon.

Tonics

Tonic water is another artificially carbonated water that has added minerals. However, it also has an extra essential ingredient that gives it a unique bitter flavour: quinine (which pairs well with gin and vodka). Originally, quinine was added to water to prevent malaria, but today's tonic water contains much lower quantities of this natural compound, which is a bark extract from the cinchona tree (*Cinchona officinalis*). Tonics are available infused with a wide range of flavours, including elderflower, pink grapefruit, damson, clementine, blood orange and rhubarb.

Sodas (Soft Drinks)

Among the options for adding fizziness to cocktails is a huge variety of soft drinks. Colas add a heavier flavour, while fizzy lemonade (lemon-flavoured soda) is a lighter option that adds a refreshing citrus flavour along with some sweetness. Rose lemonade, the most famous brand being Fentimans, contains rose oil and delivers a beautiful fragrance and pink colour. If you wish to spice up your cocktail, there's ginger ale and ginger beer. Ginger ale is sweeter and has more bubbles, but if you prefer a stronger hit of ginger that's less syrupy, ginger beer is the better choice. You may like to experiment with kombucha, which is also available in many flavours.

The Cocktail Kit

Here is the essential cocktail equipment you will need to make the drinks in this book, although many household utensils can be improvised if you don't have these to hand.

Juicer: To freshly squeeze limes, lemons, oranges and other citrus fruit, choose whichever juicer works best for you. There are hand reamers, elbow squeezers, electric juicers or just squeeze by hand!

Sharp knife: For cutting up fruit and creating garnishes.

Measure: A double-ended single / double jigger is the most useful and inexpensive investment. Singles are usually 25 ml (¾ fl oz) or 30 ml (1 fl oz). Large measures are usually 50 ml (1½ fl oz) or 60 ml (2 fl oz).

Muddler: To crush herbs, sugar, bitters and fruit, and release the aromatics, you will need a simple muddler stick with a rounded blunt end. If you don't have one, substitute the handle of a wooden spoon, or a pestle and mortar.

Cocktail shaker: A stainless steel cobbler with a built-in strainer or a Boston shaker will give you a clue as to how cold the cocktail is getting, as you shake.

Strainer: You don't really need a strainer if there is one built in, but to make the smoothest cocktails and remove any seeds or pith, keep handy both a Hawthorne strainer and a small cone-shaped bar strainer.

Mixing glass: An open-top mixing glass, which looks like a small pitcher, is great when stirring your cocktail is recommended. You can usually build these drinks in your glass, or use another glass container, but these are sturdy and won't tip over.

Stirrer: Made from metal or glass, and with a long handle for mixing ingredients, some versions come with a barspoon at one end.

Ice: You can never have enough ice. Try to keep a selection of different varieties: big cubes or spherical balls for short drinks in rocks glasses (these will melt slowly), crushed ice for tropical drinks (these will melt quickly) or small cubes to make a pretty display. Standard cubes are ideal for using in the cocktail shaker to chill your drink before discarding them.

Basic Sugar Syrup

You may like to buy a ready-made syrup to have on hand, but a basic syrup is easy to make and means you can infuse it with herbs, spices, fruit and other ingredients. If you use cup measurements, just use 1 cup of each ingredient.

240 ml (8 fl oz) water
200 g (7 oz) granulated sugar

To make the sugar syrup, bring the water to the boil in a saucepan, then add the sugar. Reduce to a simmer and stir for about 10 minutes until the sugar is dissolved. Remove from the heat, allow to cool, then strain into a clean, sealable container. Store in the refrigerator for up to 1 month.

Glassware

Many of the recipes in this book are served in a flute or coupe, glassware that retains the bubbles in your drink. The rule to keep in mind is that glasses with narrow-circumference rims retain bubbles better, and larger circumferences release aromatics. Those served in flutes, coupes and martini glasses are usually served in chilled glasses without ice, while those in rocks (old-fashioned) glasses can be served neat in a chilled glass or on the rocks. Wine glasses are great for spritzes with ice, like the Hugo. The highball is perfect for long drinks with ice, where you want the ice to dilute the drink a little. Balloons with short stems are useful for drinks over ice that you want to keep cold, and hurricanes are usually reserved for frozen drinks or those with lots of ice. Glasses are not meant to be filled to the brim, as they need the head space for swirling around or remixing if the ingredients have settled.

Liquid volumes of glassware vary according to manufacturer, so the volumes given are estimates and your particular glassware may not fall within this range.

Flute   200 ml (7 fl oz)
Useful for champagne cocktails, bellinis and mimosas, this is for chilled drinks served without ice. Hold by the stem.

Coupe   300 ml (10 fl oz)
Once the preferred glass for champagne and allegedly modelled after Marie Antoinette's breast, the coupe (or champagne saucer) is best for highly aromatic cocktails as it has a large circumference that will release scent but not retain bubbles. Usually served without ice in a chilled glass.

Wine   350 ml (12 fl oz)
A glass you are very likely to have in your home already! This is great for serving spritzes with lots of ice that include both sparkling wine and soda water (club soda), such as the Hugo or Aperol Spritz.

Martini   250 ml (9 fl oz)
Use this for chilled neat drinks without ice. The long thin stem will keep the drink away from warm hands. The V-shaped glass has a wide mouth that allows the aromatics to be released to the surface and the narrow end ensures no ingredients settle at the bottom. Obviously used for martinis, but also daiquiris and the Sidecar.

Margarita   250 ml (9 fl oz)
Like a coupe, but with a stepped shape, this is the classic glass for –
you guessed it – a margarita, but also great for a daiquiri.

Hurricane   300 ml (10 fl oz)
Often used to serve long drinks with lots of ice, frozen cocktails or
tiki drinks, this glass instantly gives a party feel to any occasion.

Balloon   400 ml (14 fl oz)
Also called the Copa de Balon, this is a traditional glass for gin and
tonics, which, with its large circumference and generous capacity,
allows the gin's aromatics to be fully released.

Rocks   Single 200 ml (7 fl oz) or double 300 ml (10 fl oz)
Often used for whiskey or whiskey-based cocktails built in the glass, it
is also called the lowball or the old-fashioned glass. Served with 'rocks'
– one or several large cubes of ice.

Highball   300–400 ml (10–14 fl oz)
Also called the Collins glass after the Tom Collins, these vary in
capacity and slimness. Great for drinks with lots of ice and height,
such as the gin fizz.

SPRING

Welcome the longer days of spring, flowers in bloom and warmer weather with these light, refreshing cocktails that use the best of seasonal ingredients. It's the perfect time of the year to enjoy fresh botanicals, herbs, fruits and floral ingredients, from lavender and lemongrass to hibiscus and rhubarb. Here you will find fizzy variations on classics such as the mint julep and Pimm's cup, as well as delicate mimosas and light spritzes.

Whether you're watching a boat race, celebrating Mother's Day, taking a spring break from work or spending a lazy afternoon with friends, these inspiring cocktails will help you make the most of every social opportunity.

Lavender Spritz

The lovely floral aroma of lavender is a wonderful way to add a touch of spring to your prosecco and the herb pairs really well with the botanicals of gin. Take advantage of the season for the fresh herb, which lasts from spring throughout the summer. If you would like a strong purple colour to your drink, substitute Empress gin for the dry gin, or add a drop of butterfly pea flower extract.

INGREDIENTS

- 30 ml (1 fl oz) dry gin
- 15 ml (½ fl oz) Lavender Syrup
- 90 ml (3 fl oz) chilled sparkling rosé wine
- Lavender sprig and blackberry, to garnish

Lavender Syrup

- 240 ml (8 fl oz) water
- 1 tablespoon fresh lavender flower buds
- 200 g (7 oz) granulated sugar

METHOD

First make the syrup. Pour the water into a saucepan and bring to the boil. Take off the heat, add the fresh lavender buds and leave to infuse for 10-15 minutes. Strain and then add the sugar and bring to a simmer. Stir for about 10 minutes until the sugar has dissolved. Remove from the heat and allow to cool.

Pour the gin and syrup into a cocktail shaker with ice. Shake well until cold, then strain into a chilled champagne flute.

Top with the sparkling rosé, garnish with a lavender sprig and a blackberry, and serve.

Yuzu Gin Fizz

Yuzu is a fragrant citrus fruit that is used most famously to make ponzu, the Japanese dipping sauce and marinade, and as a vinegar substitute in recipes. The juice adds mandarin and grapefruit flavours to this fizzy gin cocktail.

INGREDIENTS

- 30 ml (1 fl oz) yuzu juice
- 15 ml (½ fl oz) sugar syrup (see page 11)
- Dash orange bitters
- 60 ml (2 fl oz) gin
- 120 ml (4 fl oz) soda water (club soda)
- Mint sprig and yuzu or lemon slice, to garnish

METHOD

Pour the yuzu juice, sugar syrup, bitters and gin into a cocktail shaker with ice. Shake vigorously until cold, then strain into a rocks glass or tumbler filled with ice.

Top with the soda water, garnish and serve.

YUZU

With a tart, tangy and sour flavour that is reminiscent of a cross between a lemon and a grapefruit, yuzu is a yellow citrus that is excellent for including in sauces, marinades, desserts and, of course, cocktails. Available as a fruit from Japanese markets and other speciality grocers, the juice can often be found in supermarkets. It mixes well with gin and sake.

Juniper Royale

Named in honour of gin's essential botanical, this fruity sunset-coloured cocktail is saved from over-sweetness by champagne. With similar flavours to the classic Tequila Sunrise, which includes orange and grenadine, but constructed like a Kir Royale, it can also be served in a flute.

INGREDIENTS

- 30 ml (1 fl oz) dry gin
- 15 ml (½ fl oz) Juniper Syrup
- 15 ml (½ fl oz) fresh orange juice
- 15 ml (½ fl oz) cranberry juice
- Dash grenadine
- Chilled champagne, to top

Juniper Syrup

- 240 ml (8 fl oz) water
- 200 g (7 oz) granulated sugar
- 1 tablespoon crushed dried juniper berries

METHOD

First make the syrup. Bring the water to the boil in a saucepan. Add the sugar and juniper berries, reduce the heat to a simmer and stir until the sugar has dissolved. Strain and allow to cool.

Put all the ingredients, except the champagne, into a cocktail shaker with ice. Shake vigorously until cold, then strain into a chilled coupe. Top with champagne to serve.

JUNIPER BERRIES

The defining flavour of gin (in fact, the word 'gin' derives from the Dutch *jenever*, meaning 'juniper'), juniper berries are also used in Northern European cuisine and beer. In cocktails, they enhance gin's botanicals and combine well with citrus.

Hibiscus Prosecco

Beautiful and edible, whole wild hibiscus flowers in syrup add a spectacular look to a cocktail. They are easily available online and give a cranberry-like flavour. If you can't find the flowers in syrup, substitute a ready-made hibiscus simple syrup.

INGREDIENTS

- 1 hibiscus flower
- 25 ml (¾ fl oz) vodka
- 15 ml (½ fl oz) fresh orange juice
- 1 teaspoon hibiscus syrup from the jar of flowers
- Chilled rosé prosecco, to top

METHOD

Add a hibiscus flower to the bottom of a champagne flute.

Pour the vodka, orange juice and hibiscus syrup into a cocktail shaker with ice. Shake vigorously until cold, then strain into the flute. Gently pour in the rosé prosecco, watch the flower unfurl, and serve.

VARIATION

For a less alcoholic version, omit the vodka; alternatively, replace the vodka with gin.

Rhubarb Spritz

A classy take on the *Barbie* cocktail trend but with a colour more reminiscent of pastel florals than fluorescent pink! The simple spritz is given a lift here with homemade rhubarb syrup; it's worth making your own for the delicate colour and sweet fruit flavour with a hint of acidity. In winter, look for 'forced' rhubarb – it has a deeper pink hue and a sweeter taste than the summer variety.

INGREDIENTS

- 30 ml (1 fl oz) Rhubarb Syrup
- Chilled prosecco, to top
- 1 lemon wedge
- Mint sprig, to garnish

Rhubarb Syrup

- 240 ml (8 fl oz) water
- 200 g (7 oz) granulated sugar
- 250 g (9 oz) fresh rhubarb, finely chopped
- 1 vanilla pod (bean), split and seeds removed

METHOD

Make the syrup. Place the water, sugar and rhubarb in a saucepan and bring to the boil. Add the vanilla pod and reduce to a simmer for about 1 hour until the rhubarb has reduced to a mash. Strain through a fine sieve into a sealable container and keep in the refrigerator for up to 1 week.

Add the syrup to a tumbler or rocks glass filled with ice. Top with prosecco, squeeze the lemon wedge over and serve garnished with mint.

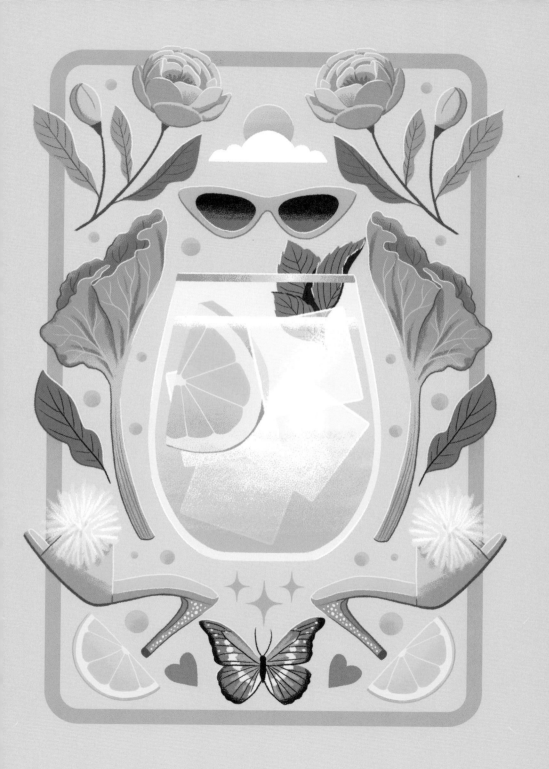

French 75

Dating from 1915, this punchy cocktail has remained popular for over a century (and inspired many a tribute recipe). The French army in World War I used 75-mm field guns – this drink is meant to have a similar kick, hence the name! Harry MacElhone of Harry's Bar in New York created one of the earliest French 75 cocktails – our version adds a touch of grenadine, which gives it a hit of fruity colour and sweetness.

INGREDIENTS

- 25 ml (¾ fl oz) gin
- 10 ml (¼ fl oz) fresh lemon juice
- Dash sugar syrup (see page 11)
- Dash grenadine
- Chilled champagne, to top
- Lemon twist, to garnish

METHOD

Place the gin, lemon juice, sugar syrup and grenadine in a cocktail shaker with ice and shake vigorously until cold.

Strain into a chilled flute and fill with champagne. Serve with a lemon twist.

VARIATION

Substitute vodka for the gin and lime juice for the lemon juice. Use a lime twist for the garnish.

Prosecco Mint Julep

Here, the traditional drink of the Kentucky Derby is given a lighter fizz treatment. It's not quite as punchy as the original, but perfect for a long afternoon watching the races. The 1862 edition of *Jerry Thomas' Bar-Tenders Guide* contains five versions of the julep, using cognac, brandy, gin or sparkling Moselle wine, as well as whiskey.

INGREDIENTS

- 6 mint leaves
- 20 ml (⅔ fl oz) sugar syrup (see page 11)
- 60 ml (2 fl oz) bourbon
- Dash Angostura bitters
- Chilled prosecco, to top
- Mint sprig, to garnish

METHOD

Build the drink in the glass. Place the mint leaves and sugar syrup in a highball glass and muddle until the mint has broken down. Add the bourbon and bitters, then fill with crushed ice. Stir gently for at least 30 seconds, until the glass gets frosty.

Top with the prosecco. Stir again gently to combine and garnish with a sprig of mint.

VARIATION

To make a peach julep version, muddle ¼ peeled and diced fresh peach with the mint in the first step and add in 20 ml (⅔ fl oz) peach liqueur with the bourbon.

Mother's Ruin

This original version of this punch was created by Phil Ward at the legendary cocktail bar Death & Co. in New York City's East Village, where it developed a cult following. Here we've adapted it using sweet vermouth infused with cinnamon tea to add a note of subtle sweetness. 'Mother's ruin' is a phrase from 1700s Britain, when cheap gin was drunk so widely that polite society worried that it was leading women into immorality.

INGREDIENTS

- 8 white sugar cubes
- 60 ml (2 fl oz) soda water (club soda)
- 120 ml (4 fl oz) gin
- 60 ml (2 fl oz) Orange Tea Vermouth
- 120 ml (4 fl oz) fresh grapefruit juice
- 60 ml (2 fl oz) fresh lemon juice
- Chilled sparkling wine of your choice, to top
- Grapefruit slices, to garnish

Orange Tea Vermouth

- 45 g (½ oz) orange and cinnamon spiced tea leaves
- 130 ml (4 fl oz) sweet vermouth

METHOD

To make the orange tea vermouth, add the tea leaves to the vermouth and let stand for 2 hours. Strain through a fine sieve and store in the refrigerator for up to 1 month.

In a jug, muddle the sugar cubes with the soda water until broken up and dissolved. Add the gin, orange tea vermouth and grapefruit and lemon juices. Add ice cubes and stir until chilled.

Pour into individual rocks glasses over ice, top with the sparkling wine and garnish with grapefruit slices.

Paloma Mimosa

A delicious cocktail that is bursting with flavours, the Paloma Mimosa is a fancier take on the orange juice used in the classic buck's fizz (orange mimosa). It makes an elegant drink for a wedding or anniversary brunch, a bridal shower or as a Mother's Day treat.

INGREDIENTS

- 30 ml (1 fl oz) fresh grapefruit juice
- 60 ml (2 fl oz) tequila
- 10 ml (¼ fl oz) fresh lime juice
- Chilled champagne or prosecco, to top
- Lime and grapefruit wedges, to garnish

For the rim

- 1 tablespoon granulated sugar
- 1 tablespoon sea salt

METHOD

Prepare the rim decoration by stirring together the sugar and salt in a saucer. Wet the rim of a champagne flute with a lime wedge and dip in the mixture to coat.

In a cocktail shaker, combine the grapefruit juice, tequila and lime juice with ice. Shake well until cold, strain into the flute and top with the champagne. Garnish with lime and grapefruit and serve.

VARIATION

For a longer drink with a brighter colour, add 30 ml (1 fl oz) of blood orange juice or grenadine and serve over ice in a highball.

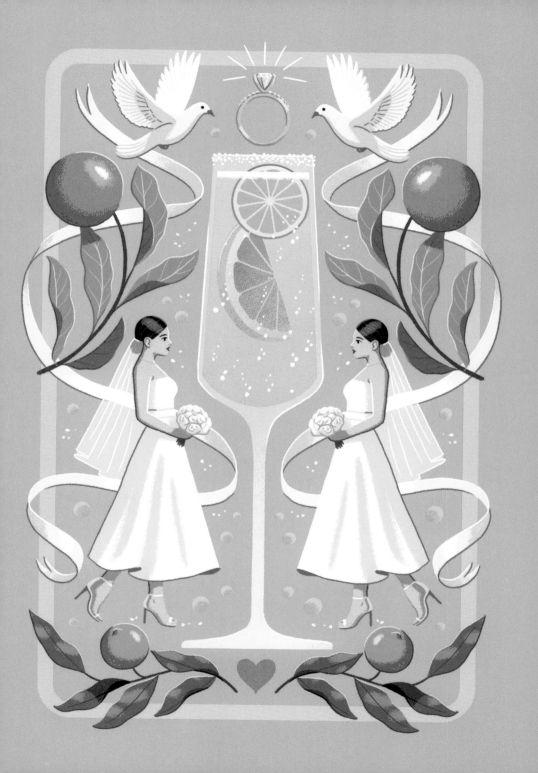

Lychee Mai Tai

A blend of Polynesian and Caribbean influences, the Mai Tai is the quintessential tiki bar drink. Created by Victor Jules Bergeron, known as Trader Vic, in Hawaii in the 1940s, the drink reputedly got its name when a customer declared 'Mai Tai-Roa Aé' upon drinking it – roughly translated from Tahitian as 'Out of this world, the best'. Since then, many variations have followed, including this one with lychee, as well as guava and mango versions.

INGREDIENTS

- 90 ml (3 fl oz) Lychee Purée
- 30 ml (1 fl oz) dark rum
- 30 ml (1 fl oz) white rum
- 15 ml (½ fl oz) amaretto
- 15 ml (½ oz) Cointreau
- 1 tablespoon sugar syrup (see page 11)
- ½ lime
- Soda water (club soda), to top
- Mint sprig, lime wedge and lychee, to garnish

Lychee Purée

- 90 ml (3 fl oz) lychee juice
- 5 lychee fruit (tinned)

METHOD

First make the purée. Combine the lychee juice and fruit in a blender and process until smooth.

Transfer to a cocktail shaker, add the dark and white rum, amaretto, Cointreau and sugar syrup. Squeeze in the juice from the lime. Add ice and shake vigorously until cold.

Double strain into a hurricane glass filled with crushed ice and top with the soda water. Thread the mint, lime wedge and a lychee on to a cocktail stick to garnish, and serve.

Lemongrass Rosé

This Thai-inspired cocktail is made with a herby lemongrass sugar syrup, which also combines well with gin and ginger beer if you would like to switch it up. You could even infuse your vodka with a few stalks of lemongrass if you really enjoy the floral lemony taste.

INGREDIENTS

- 30 ml (1 fl oz) lemon vodka
- 15 ml (½ fl oz) St Germain elderflower liqueur
- 15 ml (½ fl oz) Lemongrass Syrup
- 15 ml (½ fl oz) fresh lemon juice
- Chilled sparkling rosé wine, to top
- Lemongrass stalk and an orchid flower, to garnish

Lemongrass Syrup

- 240 ml (8 fl oz) water
- 200 g (7 oz) granulated sugar
- 6–8 stalks lemongrass, roughly chopped

METHOD

Add all the syrup ingredients to a saucepan and bring to the boil. Reduce to a simmer and stir for about 15 minutes, until the sugar has dissolved. Remove from the heat and infuse for 30 minutes. Strain into a sealable container.

Add the vodka, elderflower liqueur, syrup and lemon juice to a cocktail shaker with ice. Shake vigorously until cold, then strain into a chilled coupe glass.

Top with the sparkling rosé and garnish with a lemongrass stalk and the flower.

VARIATIONS

Add 1 tablespoon grated ginger to the lemongrass syrup recipe for a spicier flavour. Add 5–7 mint leaves to the syrup for a refreshing taste.

Ramos Tequila Fizz

A variation on the classic Ramos gin fizz, which was created in New Orleans in 1888 by bar owner Henry Charles Ramos, this one is based on tequila and is just as creamy, fluffy and citrussy. Legend has it that the original, reputedly a favourite of Louisiana Governor Huey Long, took 12 minutes to shake properly. See the variation on page 96 to make the original version.

INGREDIENTS

- 50 ml (1½ fl oz) reposado tequila
- 15 ml (½ fl oz) fresh lemon juice
- 15 ml (½ fl oz) fresh lime juice
- 30 ml (1 fl oz) orange flower water
- 30 ml (1 fl oz) sugar syrup (see page 11)
- 50 ml (1½ fl oz) double (heavy) cream
- 1 egg white
- Soda water (club soda), to top
- Lime wedge, to garnish

METHOD

Combine all the ingredients except the soda water and garnish in a cocktail shaker without ice and dry shake robustly for 60 seconds. If the cream splits, the shaking will emulsify and merge the ingredients.

Add ice and shake for a further 60 seconds until cold. Simultaneously and slowly, pour two-thirds of the ingredients and the soda water into a chilled highball glass from a height, until the head rises above the glass.

Leave for 30 seconds, preferably in the refrigerator, for the head to settle, then poke a hole in the top and pour in the remaining cocktail. Garnish and serve.

Strawberry Pimms Cup

A traditional drink for boat races and tennis, Pimms is given a fruity twist by blending it with fresh strawberries. This pink drink packs a punch, so if you prefer a less alcoholic version, substitute sparkling pink lemonade, such as Fentimans, for the sparkling rosé wine.

INGREDIENTS

- 4 fresh strawberries
- 1 teaspoon sugar syrup (see page 11)
- 50 ml (1½ fl oz) Pimm's No.1
- 1 tablespoon fresh lemon juice
- 1 drop vanilla extract
- 3 mint leaves
- 1 orange slice
- 1 cucumber ribbon
- 1 strawberry, halved
- Sparkling rosé wine, to top
- Mint sprig and strawberry, to garnish

METHOD

Muddle the strawberries in a cocktail shaker. Add the sugar syrup, Pimms, lemon juice and vanilla extract, and shake with ice until very cold.

Fill a jar or tumbler with the mint leaves, orange, cucumber, strawberry and ice, then strain the strawberry Pimms into the glass.

Top with sparkling rosé. Stir gently to combine. Garnish with mint and strawberry.

French Blonde Spritz

This sparkling version of the floral and citrus cocktail, reputedly a favourite of singer Taylor Swift, is deliciously light, delicate and refreshing. Lillet Blanc works beautifully with bubbles, imparting a flavour profile of candied oranges, honey and exotic fruit. Choose a highly botanical gin for this recipe.

INGREDIENTS

- 60 ml (2 fl oz) Lillet Blanc
- 60 ml (2 fl oz) fresh grapefruit juice
- 30 ml (1 fl oz) gin
- 30 ml (1 fl oz) St Germain elderflower liqueur
- Soda water (club soda), to top
- Lemon twist and grapefruit slice, to garnish

METHOD

Pour the Lillet Blanc, grapefruit juice, gin and elderflower liqueur in a cocktail shaker with ice. Shake vigorously to combine. Pour over ice into a wine glass and top with soda water.

Stir gently and serve garnished with the lemon and grapefruit.

VARIATION

Substitute pink grapefruit juice and Lillet Rosé for the yellow and blanc versions to make a French Redhead.

Sgroppino

Created in medieval Venice, this slushy, sorbet-based cocktail was traditionally served to cleanse the palate between courses and help digestion. Sgroppino means 'to unwind', and the dessert-like drink is bright, lemony and perfect for a warm day.

INGREDIENTS

- 1 scoop lemon sorbet
- 30 ml (1 fl oz) lemon vodka
- 90 ml (3 fl oz) chilled prosecco
- Lemon zest, lemon slice and mint sprig, to garnish

METHOD

Place the sorbet in a metal mixing bowl, add the vodka and whisk until smooth. Add the prosecco and whisk again lightly to combine. Pour into a chilled margarita glass.

Scatter the lemon zest over the top, add the lemon slice and mint, and serve.

VARIATION

Substitute plain vodka for the lemon, peach sorbet for the lemon sorbet and garnish with a fresh peach slice.

Butterfly Pea Cocktail

Using butterfly pea flower extract is easy way to make an eye-catching, colour-changing cocktail, but if you can only find the dried flowers then steep them in the gin overnight before straining. The lemon juice transforms the blue extract into a beautiful purple colour.

INGREDIENTS

- 50 ml (1½ fl oz) gin
- 30 ml (1 fl oz) fresh lemon juice
- 25 ml (¾ fl oz) runny honey
- 15 ml (½ fl oz) crème de violette
- 15 ml (½ fl oz) Cointreau
- Chilled prosecco, to top
- 2 drops butterfly pea flower extract
- Lemon slice, to garnish

METHOD

Pour the gin, lemon juice, honey, crème de violette and Cointreau into a cocktail shaker with ice. Shake vigorously until cold.

Pour over ice into a rocks glass and top with prosecco. Add the butterfly pea flower extract and watch the colour change! If you want a deeper colour, add another drop of the extract. Garnish with a lemon slice.

CRÈME DE VIOLETTE

Also known as violet liqueur, the drink dates from the early nineteenth century in Europe when it was served as a cordial. Made by macerating violet flowers in brandy, it has a sweet, floral, candy-like taste and a bright purple colour.

SUMMER

Indulge in the height of summer's fresh fruit with cocktails that include juicy watermelon, mango, passion fruit and pineapple, as well as raspberries and strawberries that are bursting with flavour. Discover the cooling combination of cucumber and mint or the delicate floral taste of elderflower. Decorate your drinks with edible flowers, basil strips, mint leaves, melon balls and citrus slices.

Rum- and tequila-based drinks will transport you to tropical islands, even if you never leave your neighbourhood, while a sip of limoncello will send you to the Amalfi coast. And for icy treats to cool off on hot days, try the Frozen Peach Bellini or Pineapple Frosecco.

Watermelon Sugar

Super refreshing and vibrant, this summertime drink will get the barbecue or picnic started, and it is easy to scale up for jugs. Swap out the prosecco for soda water (club soda) for a less potent mix. You could use a melon-baller to create watermelon balls for the garnish.

INGREDIENTS

- 150 g (5 oz) seedless watermelon, rind removed
- 15 ml (½ fl oz) fresh lime juice
- 2 teaspoons sugar syrup (see page 11)
- 50 ml (1½ fl oz) blanco tequila
- 50 ml (1½ fl oz) chilled prosecco
- Watermelon and lime wedges, to garnish

METHOD

Place the watermelon, lime juice and sugar syrup in a blender and blitz for about 5 seconds until puréed. Strain through a fine sieve into a mixing glass, add the tequila and stir. Carefully pour in the prosecco and gently stir.

Pour into a tumbler with ice, garnish with the watermelon and lime wedges, and serve.

WATERMELON

The juice, purée and sugar syrup of the watermelon has become a popular ingredient for summer cocktails as it pairs well with clear spirits, lime, mint, strawberries and cranberry juice. It also adds a punchy colour and refreshing flavour.

Serves 1

Cucumber Sparkler

A vodka-based drink for a hot day and a great choice for any gardener with a glut of cucumbers (or vodka). Cucumber and mint are both cooling ingredients – you could muddle a little mint with the cucumber and lime juice for an extra hit of mint in the glass. You could also make this with soda water (club soda) or sparkling water instead of the sparkling wine for a lower alcohol drink.

INGREDIENTS

- 1 or 2 long cucumber ribbons, soaked in vodka for 30 minutes
- 2.5 cm (1 inch) piece of cucumber, peeled and chopped
- 15 ml (½ fl oz) fresh lime juice
- 50 ml (1½ fl oz) vodka
- 15 ml (½ fl oz) elderflower cordial
- Chilled sparkling wine of your choice, to top
- Mint sprig, to garnish

METHOD

Wrap the vodka-marinated cucumber ribbons around the inside of a tumbler and fill with ice.

Muddle together the chopped cucumber and lime juice in a cocktail shaker. Add the vodka, elderflower cordial and ice.

Shake well until cold and strain into the prepared tumbler. Top with the sparkling wine and garnish with a mint sprig.

VARIATION

Thread the vodka-soaked cucumber ribbon on a cocktail stick with the mint to make a garnish.

Serves 1

Strawberry Pisco Fizz

A sweet take on a Pisco Sour with strawberry purée adding a gorgeous colour, and the all-important egg white foam top. You can buy edible flowers in large supermarkets in season or grow your own (wash before using and let dry on kitchen paper). If you can't find fresh edible flowers, try freeze-dried strawberry pieces or dried rose petals as decoration, or cut a whole small strawberry almost in half and wedge it on the rim of the glass.

INGREDIENTS

- 30 ml (1 fl oz) pisco
- 30 ml (1 fl oz) fresh lemon juice
- 30 ml (1 fl oz) Strawberry Purée (see page 66)
- 1 teaspoon vanilla syrup
- 1 egg white
- 30 ml (1 fl oz) chilled prosecco
- Edible flowers, such as violet and pansy, to serve

METHOD

Add the pisco, lemon juice, strawberry purée, vanilla syrup and egg white to a cocktail shaker with ice and shake until cold.

Pour the prosecco into a coupe glass and strain over the cocktail mixture. Let the egg white foam settle before garnishing with the edible flowers.

PISCO

With an herbaceous floral taste that is compared to grappa, pisco is a Peruvian (some claim Chilean) unaged brandy made by fermenting grapes. Most famously, it is used in the Pisco Sour, made with orange flower water, lime and egg white.

Melon Ball Blast

This fun drink is halfway between a sundae and a cocktail – serve it with a cocktail stick on the side so you can spear the melon balls. For best effect, make sure you use the three varieties of melon with their contrasting colours and flavours. The chiffonade of fresh basil strips adds a glorious fragrance to each sip and offsets the intense sweetness of the melon.

INGREDIENTS

- 180 g (6 oz) honeydew, watermelon and cantaloupe balls, scooped using a melon baller
- 15 ml (½ fl oz) crème de menthe
- 15 ml (½ fl oz) fresh lime juice
- 1 teaspoon sugar syrup (see page 11)
- Chilled sparkling wine of your choice, to top
- 2 fresh basil leaves
- Mint sprig, to garnish

METHOD

Place the melon balls in a large bowl and add the crème de menthe. Stir well to combine and let stand for 1 hour. Mix the lime juice and sugar syrup and add to the melon.

Just before serving, spoon the melon balls into a balloon glass and top with the sparkling wine.

Stack the basil leaves and roll them tightly, then cut them crosswise into thin ribbons (this is a chiffonade; cutting the basil roughly will discolour the leaves). Top with the basil ribbons, garnish with a mint sprig and serve.

Raspberry Limoncello

The combination of lemon and raspberry is a flavour match made in heaven. Limoncello is traditionally served as an after-dinner digestif, but its sweetness can be a little overpowering; here the prosecco or soda water makes the perfect softener. It's also a great way to use that bottle of limoncello you may have brought home from a holiday in Italy!

INGREDIENTS
- 5 raspberries
- 30 ml (1 fl oz) vodka
- 30 ml (1 fl oz) limoncello
- 15 ml (½ fl oz) fresh lemon juice
- Chilled prosecco or soda water (club soda), to top
- Mint sprig, raspberries and lemon slice, to garnish

METHOD

Place the raspberries in a cocktail shaker and muddle. Fill with ice and add the vodka, limoncello and lemon juice. Shake vigorously until cold, then double strain into a wine glass filled with ice.

Top with the prosecco or soda water, garnish and serve.

LIMONCELLO

Limoncello was patented in Capri, Italy, in 1988 and is made from the Amalfi region's abundance of high-grade lemons, steeped in vodka. Store it in the fridge or freezer, so its cooling and refreshing flavour can be enjoyed on the spot.

Barracuda

Created in the late 1950s by an Italian cruise-ship bartender, Benito Cuppari, the Barracuda is traditionally served in a pineapple shell. Cuppari named it after a friend's beach club, the Barracuda, in Portofino, which was a popular celebrity nightspot. This version of the tropical drink adds grenadine for a touch of pomegranate flavour, but purists can feel free to omit it.

INGREDIENTS

- 30 ml (1 fl oz) dark rum
- 30 ml (1 fl oz) Galliano
- 30 ml (1 fl oz) pineapple juice
- 15 ml (½ fl oz) fresh lime juice
- 15 ml (½ fl oz) grenadine (optional)
- Chilled prosecco, to top
- Pineapple wedge and frond, to garnish

METHOD

Pour the rum, Galliano, pineapple juice, lime juice and grenadine into a cocktail shaker with ice. Shake vigorously until cold, then strain into a chilled margarita glass.

Top with the prosecco, garnish with the pineapple wedge and frond, and serve.

VARIATION

For a special garnish, and to bring out the flavour, char the pineapple wedge with a kitchen blowtorch.

The Hugo

The cocktail was conceived in 2005 by bar manager Roland Gruber (aka A.K.) at San Zeno Bar in Tyrol, Italy, as an alternative to Spritz Veneziano, made with bitters and prosecco. Initially, the recipe provided for the use of lemon balm cordial, which was then replaced by the more easily available elderflower cordial (syrup). This version uses gin to pair with the herbal notes, but for a more classic version, leave the gin out. Refreshing and floral, the Hugo is a perfect drink for warm summer evenings.

INGREDIENTS

- Small handful of mint leaves, plus 1 mint sprig, to garnish
- 20 ml (⅔ fl oz) elderflower cordial
- 30 ml (1 fl oz) dry gin
- 30 ml (1 fl oz) soda water (club soda)
- 120 ml (4 fl oz) chilled prosecco
- Lime wedge, to garnish

METHOD

Gently scrunch the mint in your hands to lightly bruise it, then place at the bottom of a large wine or spritz glass. Pour in the elderflower cordial and gin and leave to infuse for 1–2 minutes.

Fill the glass with ice, then pour over the soda water and prosecco. Stir gently to combine. Garnish with the lime and mint.

ELDERFLOWER CORDIAL

Adding a sweet, delicate, floral flavour to drinks, elderflower mixes well with sparkling wines, as well as gin and vodka. Available as a non-alcoholic cordial (syrup) or as an alcoholic liqueur, either can be used in the recipes in this book.

Colletti Royale

The margarita gets an upgrade here, with tequila and lime making a base for a long drink with complex orange and flower notes and finished with champagne. The original Colletti Royale was created by mixologist Julie Reiner, co-owner of the celebrated cocktail bars Clover Club and Leyenda in New York City. Ours is distinctly upmarket, made with reposado tequila (which is aged for up to a year) and rosé champagne; for a more economical version, use your standard blanco (silver) tequila and fizz of choice.

INGREDIENTS

- 50 ml (1½ fl oz) reposado tequila
- 15 ml (½ fl oz) Cointreau
- 15 ml (½ fl oz) St Germain elderflower liqueur
- 15 ml (½ fl oz) fresh blood orange juice
- 15 ml (½ fl oz) fresh lime juice
- 2 dashes orange bitters
- Chilled sparkling rosé wine, to top
- Blood orange slice, to garnish

METHOD

Add the tequila, Cointreau, elderflower liqueur, blood orange juice, lime juice and bitters to a cocktail shaker with ice and shake vigorously until cold. Strain into a chilled margarita glass.

Top with the sparkling rosé wine and garnish with the orange slice.

Serves 1

Summer Strawberry Sparkler

A pretty cocktail with light sweetness and a base note of brandy, this is best made in the summer months when both strawberries and sparkling rosé wine are at their best. Like a bubbly version of a daiquiri, you could make this with rum instead of the cognac.

INGREDIENTS

- 30 ml (1 fl oz) cognac
- 25 ml (¾ fl oz) fresh lemon juice
- 25 ml (¾ fl oz) Strawberry Purée
- Dash rosewater
- 50 ml (1½ fl oz) chilled sparkling rosé wine
- Fresh strawberry and dried rose petals, to garnish

Strawberry Purée

- 200 g (7 oz) hulled and chopped strawberries
- 1 tablespoon granulated sugar
- Dash of fresh lemon juice

METHOD

To make the strawberry purée, combine all the ingredients in a blender and blitz until smooth.

Pass through a sieve into a sealable container. It will keep in the fridge for 2–3 days.

Pour the cognac, lemon juice, purée and rosewater in a cocktail shaker with ice. Shake vigorously until cold. Strain into a rocks glass or tumbler over ice and top with the sparkling rosé wine.

Garnish with the strawberry and rose petals, and serve.

Frozen Peach Bellini

Invented sometime in the 1940s by the owner of Harry's Bar in Venice, Giuseppe Cipriani, the bellini has spread around the world. This version includes peach for extra depth of flavour and recreates the classic as a slushy that could be served as a dessert (you can buy ready-frozen peach slices at the supermarket). To retain the blush-pink look of the original cocktail, add a few fresh raspberries to the blender.

INGREDIENTS

- 225 g (8 oz) frozen sliced peaches
- 15 ml (½ fl oz) sugar syrup (see page 11)
- 50 ml (1½ fl oz) peach liqueur
- 240 ml (8 fl oz) chilled prosecco
- Peach slice, to garnish

METHOD

Place the frozen peaches, sugar syrup, peach liqueur and prosecco in a blender and pulse until it becomes a slush. Pour into a chilled coupe and decorate with a fresh peach slice.

PEACH LIQUEUR

You will find this liqueur under the names of peach schnapps, peach brandy and crème de pêche. Whichever one you choose, make sure it is made with real fruit instead of just flavourings. The scent should be bright, fruity and fresh.

Pineapple Frosecco

The combination of rum and pineapple is one that needs no introduction, but when you add frozen prosecco you've got some welcome acidity to counteract the sweetness of the pineapple and a refreshing sorbet vibe. You'll need to start the night before for this one, so why not scale up for a crowd as suggested below? It's a holiday in a glass – cocktail umbrella optional!

INGREDIENTS

- 150 ml (5 fl oz) prosecco
- 225 g (8 oz) fresh pineapple chunks
- 15 ml (½ fl oz) pineapple juice
- 15 ml (½ fl oz) rum
- 15 ml (½ fl oz) sugar syrup (see page 11)
- Pineapple wedge and maraschino cherry, to garnish

METHOD

Freeze the prosecco overnight in an ice cube tray. The alcohol will prevent the prosecco from freezing completely, but the slushy effect is the desired result.

Place the frozen prosecco cubes in a blender with 3 ice cubes. Add the pineapple chunks, pineapple juice, rum and sugar syrup and process on high until blended.

Serve immediately in a hurricane glass garnished with a pineapple wedge and a maraschino cherry.

The Passion

The legendary mixologist Chris Edwardes, the former bartender of the Groucho Club in London, is credited with devising this cocktail with its tropical flavours that combine passion fruit and peach. If you are a fan of the Porn-Star Martini, this is one for you.

INGREDIENTS

- 30 ml (1 fl oz) rum
- 15 ml (½ fl oz) peach liqueur
- 1 tablespoon fresh lime juice
- 15 ml (½ fl oz) sugar syrup (see page 11)
- 1 passion fruit or 30 ml (1 fl oz) ready-made passion fruit purée
- Sparkling wine of your choice, to top
- Splash soda water (club soda)
- Mint sprig, to garnish

METHOD

Add the rum, peach liqueur, lime juice and sugar syrup with ice to a cocktail shaker. Shake vigorously until cold. Strain into a highball filled with ice.

Scoop the flesh of the passion fruit into the glass or use a premade passion fruit purée.

Stir well, then top with the sparkling wine and a splash of soda water. Garnish with the mint sprig and serve.

PASSION FRUIT

With its sweet, tart flavour and crunchy seeds, the passion fruit is the perfect ingredient for a margarita, mojito, daiquiri or caipirinha recipe. Choose heavy, dark-purple coloured fruit; these indicate ripeness and a good amount of pulp.

La Dolce Vita

A drink to celebrate the good life! While there are several cocktails with this name, some including Cointreau or Campari, this variation celebrates the Italian grapes at the heart of prosecco. It makes a fresh and light summertime drink.

INGREDIENTS

- 5 seedless green or white grapes
- 1 teaspoon honey
- 30 ml (1 fl oz) vodka
- Dash orange bitters
- Chilled prosecco, to top
- Lemon twist, to garnish

METHOD

Place the grapes and honey in a cocktail shaker and muddle well until the grapes break down and release their juice. Add the vodka and bitters and shake vigorously with ice until cold.

Strain into a chilled martini glass, top with prosecco and serve with a lemon twist.

PROSECCO GRAPES

For a boozy garnish or snack, steep 240 g (8 oz) of green or white grapes in 240 ml (8 fl oz) prosecco, 30 ml (1 fl oz) vodka and 1 teaspoon sugar syrup. Cover and chill overnight. The next day, strain the grapes and roll them in sugar.

Bombay Bellini

A peach bellini with an exotic mango twist! Make your own purée by simply blitzing fresh ripe fruit chunks in a blender until smooth. You can pass it through a sieve to remove any pulp and fibres if you like. The purée freezes well and can be added to smoothies, desserts, or a frozen margarita or daiquiri.

INGREDIENTS

- 180 ml (6 fl oz) fresh white peach purée
- Dash peach brandy
- Dash fresh lemon juice
- 60 ml (2 fl oz) fresh mango purée
- Chilled sparkling wine of your choice, to top
- Mango slice and mint sprig, to serve

METHOD

Stir the peach purée, peach brandy and lemon juice in a chilled champagne flute.

Spoon in the mango purée and then slowly top up with the sparkling wine. Garnish with the mango and mint, and serve.

MANGO

First grown 5,000 years ago in India, the mango has a delicious, sweet, tropical flavour that marries well with coconut, lime, pineapple, peach and banana. It pairs with rum, tequila and Cointreau in cocktails.

Aperol Spritz

Originally created in Padua, Italy, in 1919, this refreshing bittersweet drink consists of bitters (the Aperol), prosecco and soda water and has become the go-to summertime drink. Aperol is made from an infusion of herbs and roots, including bitter and sweet oranges and rhubarb. It is often described as the less alcoholic version of Campari.

INGREDIENTS

- 60 ml (2 fl oz) Aperol
- 90 ml (3 fl oz) chilled prosecco
- 15 ml (½ fl oz) clementine or orange-flavoured tonic water
- Clementine or orange slice, to garnish

METHOD

Pour the Aperol into a wine glass filled with ice. Add the prosecco, gently stir, and top with the tonic water. Garnish with the clementine slice and serve.

VARIATIONS

VARIATION 1: Swap the prosecco for a sparkling rosé wine and the tonic for passion fruit juice to make a rosé version.

VARIATION 2: Swap the Aperol for limoncello, replace the tonic water with soda water (club soda) and use a lemon slice instead of a clementine as a garnish.

VARIATION 3: For a Japanese Sake Spritz, swap the prosecco for sake and the tonic for yuzu juice.

Blue Paradise

Reminiscent of the clear blue waters of tropical beaches, and a fizzy take on the Blue Hawaiian, this drink omits the vodka and adds Cointreau for a more concentratedly orange flavour. Made since 1912, curaçao is flavoured with the laraha orange peel, a type of orange that grows on the island of Curaçao in the Caribbean.

INGREDIENTS

- 30 ml (1 fl oz) blue curaçao
- 30 ml (1 fl oz) Cointreau
- 30 ml (1 fl oz) fresh lemon juice
- Chilled sparkling wine of your choice, to top
- Lemon twist and orange slice, to garnish

METHOD

Pour the blue curaçao, Cointreau and lemon juice into a cocktail shaker with ice. Shake vigorously until cold, then strain into a highball glass filled with ice. Top with the sparkling wine.

Garnish with the lemon twist and orange slice, and serve.

VARIATION

For a seriously more potent hit, add 15 ml (½ fl oz) vodka – or for a lighter drink, swap soda water (club soda) for the sparkling wine.

Drunken Mermaid

A tropical rum-based drink that will put you in the mood for taking a dip in the pool or ocean, this cocktail blends rum, curaçao, melon liqueur and pineapple for a tropical powerhouse concoction. With its seafoam colour, this is a fun drink for sitting in a tiki hut on the beach, or just pretending you are!

INGREDIENTS

- 60 ml (2 fl oz) white rum
- 30 ml (1 fl oz) blue curaçao
- 30 ml (1 fl oz) Midori
- 30 ml (1 fl oz) pineapple juice
- 60 ml (2 fl oz) soda water (club soda)
- Chilled prosecco, to top
- Pineapple wedge and maraschino cherry, to garnish

METHOD

Add the rum, blue curaçao, Midori and pineapple juice to a cocktail shaker with ice. Shake well until cold, then strain over ice into a balloon glass.

Top with the soda water and prosecco. Garnish with a pineapple wedge and a cherry. Cocktail umbrella optional!

MIDORI

This bright green muskmelon-flavoured liqueur originated in Japan, became popular in the 1970s. Very sweet, it is often included in tropical cocktails where its robust flavour stands up amid other strong ingredients.

Pineapple-Coconut Blast

An attractive, creamy, cold drink that refreshes on a hot day, this will transport you to the South Seas! Rather than the lighter touch that fruity tropical drinks deliver, this is a tiki-bar cocktail with a base of robust flavour and texture. Serve in a coconut shell for the full experience!

INGREDIENTS

- 60 ml (2 fl oz) coconut milk
- 60 ml (2 fl oz) fresh pineapple juice
- 60 ml (2 fl oz) white rum
- 125 g (4½ oz) frozen pineapple chunks
- Chilled prosecco, to top
- Lime wedge, to garnish

For the rim

- Shredded coconut
- Lime wedge

METHOD

Prepare the glass. Place the shredded coconut on a plate. Run the lime wedge around the rim of a margarita glass and dip in the coconut.

Add the coconut milk, pineapple juice, rum and frozen pineapple to a blender and process until smooth. Pour into the glass and top with the prosecco. Garnish with a lime wedge and serve.

PINEAPPLE

No other ingredient is as essential to tropical or tiki cocktail-making than the pineapple. Fresh, frozen or as juice, the rich fruity flavour is complemented by an acidity that harmonizes with spicy rum, lime and coconut.

AUTUMN

Usher in the cooler weather with cocktails that make the most of autumn and orchard fruits, such as apple, fig and pear, as well as warming ginger, fragrant rosemary, comforting vanilla and sweet maple syrup.

Apple and cherry brandy, blackberry and blackcurrant liqueurs, blueberry syrup and maraschino add deep, rich fruitiness to fizzy, celebratory drinks. Relax with the evocatively named Ombre Bramble, perfect after a walk in the country, or sip the Pumpkin Spice Fizz if you love that seasonal flavour. The Apple Sangria is a great party punch for a Halloween party or a bonfire night.

Ombre Bramble

This striking cocktail is based on a simple Tom Collins with the addition of blackberry flavours. Let the base mixture settle in the glass and pour your fizz over really slowly so that you create two distinct layers of colour. You can also use the rosemary sprig to swirl the two layers together.

INGREDIENTS

- 30 ml (1 fl oz) gin
- 15 ml (½ fl oz) fresh lemon juice
- 1 teaspoon sugar syrup (see page 11)
- 10 ml (¼ fl oz) blackberry liqueur
- Chilled prosecco or soda water (club soda), to top
- 2 blackberries and a rosemary sprig, to garnish

METHOD

Add the gin, lemon juice, sugar syrup and blackberry liqueur to a cocktail shaker with ice and shake vigorously until cold.

Strain into a chilled flute and wait for the mixture to settle at the bottom of the glass. Then top carefully with prosecco or soda water, pouring it over the spoon so it layers. Drizzle a little extra blackberry liqueur over the top if desired. Garnish and serve.

VARIATION

Instead of blackberry liqueur, use blackberry sugar syrup and omit the sugar syrup in the recipe.

Pomegranate Smash

Pomegranates have been grown for thousands of years and are rich in symbolic meaning in many cultures. The seeds have a sweet, tart flavour and distinct texture. You can buy the seeds in the supermarket, but if you've got a fresh fruit, cut it in half across the middle and hold one half over a bowl. Hit the skin with a wooden spoon or rolling pin and the seeds should drop out. You can then use the resulting fresh juice in your smash, too.

INGREDIENTS

- 60 ml (2 fl oz) pomegranate juice
- 1 teaspoon maple syrup
- 30 ml (1 fl oz) vodka
- 1 teaspoon crème de cassis
- Chilled prosecco, to top
- 1 tablespoon pomegranate seeds
- Mint sprig, to garnish

METHOD

Place the pomegranate juice, maple syrup, vodka and crème de cassis in a cocktail shaker with ice and shake vigorously until cold.

Strain into a tumbler or rocks glass filled with crushed ice and top with prosecco. Drop in the pomegranate seeds, garnish with a sprig of mint and serve.

MAPLE SYRUP

Turn your cocktail into an autumnal serve by using maple syrup for the sweetener. Agave syrup and sugar are wonderful for more neutral cocktails, but the caramel richness of maple syrup highlights fruit brandies, bourbon and rum.

Ritz Fizz

The origin story of this boldly coloured drink is that it was created at the Ritz-Carlton hotel in Boston in 1934, one of many new recipes created to celebrate the end of Prohibition in the United States. Curaçao, made with bitter orange peel, and lemon juice add a citrussy layer to the drink to balance the sweet amaretto. Curaçao's blue colour is artificial – but it's a fun look for a themed party.

INGREDIENTS

- 15 ml (½ fl oz) amaretto
- 15 ml (½ fl oz) blue curaçao
- 15 ml (½ fl oz) fresh lemon juice
- Chilled prosecco or champagne, to top
- Lemon twist, to garnish

METHOD

Pour the first three ingredients into a chilled flute, stir, then top with chilled prosecco or champagne.

Garnish with a lemon twist and serve.

CURAÇAO

Most famous for its inclusion in the kitsch classic the Blue Hawaiian, curaçao is a highly fragrant liqueur based on the aromatic oil of bitter oranges known as laraha, from the island of Curaçao, near Aruba.

The Duke

A refreshing long drink with layers of citrus flavours and bitters, topped with champagne (the Duke will accept no substitute for the real thing). Egg white is used in cocktails to add an attractive foamy top, but here, a whole egg imparts a richer flavour and smoothness to the base. The maraschino liqueur imparts a gorgeous colour. Make sure you use a really fresh egg for this one (a fresh egg will sink in a bowl of water; an older one will float).

INGREDIENTS

- 1 small egg
- 15 ml (½ fl oz) Cointreau
- ½ teaspoon maraschino liqueur
- 2 teaspoons fresh lemon juice
- 2 teaspoons fresh orange juice
- Chilled champagne, to top
- Lemon twist, to garnish

METHOD

Crack the whole egg into a cocktail shaker. Add the Cointreau, maraschino liqueur and lemon and orange juices and dry shake to emulsify; you want to achieve a smooth mixture, so you may need to shake for over 1 minute. Then add ice and shake again until cold.

Strain into a flute, slowly top with the champagne, then garnish with a lemon twist and serve.

VARIATION

For a brighter colour and a sweeter, more tropical taste, substitute the orange juice with blood orange juice.

Foaming Gin Fizz

Similar to a sour, a fizz features a spirit with a citrus, a sugar and a sparkling water, often with an egg white, which creates a frothy, bubbly concoction. For this cocktail, you need to dry-shake first to help the liquid ingredients merge with the egg white. You can also serve this over ice.

INGREDIENTS

- 60 ml (2 fl oz) gin
- 30 ml (1 fl oz) fresh lemon juice
- 25 ml (¾ fl oz) sugar syrup (see page 11)
- 1 egg white
- Chilled soda water (club soda), to top
- Lemon twist and mint, to garnish

METHOD

Add the gin, lemon juice, sugar syrup and egg white to a cocktail shaker and dry shake vigorously without ice for about 15 seconds.

Add 4–5 ice cubes to the shaker and shake again until cold. Double strain into a chilled highball glass. Very carefully top with the soda water, so the foam rises but doesn't overflow. Garnish and serve.

VARIATION

To make a Ramos Gin Fizz, substitute 15 ml (½ fl oz) each of lime and lemon juice for the lemon juice. Add 30 ml (1 fl oz) single (light) cream and 3 drops orange blossom water to the shaker.

Figgy Fizz

A beautiful pink drink with the rich, autumnal flavours of fig makes this a stand-out selection for celebrations. The homemade sugar syrup can be adjusted as you like – add more fruit if you love the deep bold taste.

INGREDIENTS

- 50 ml (1½ fl oz) vodka
- 15 ml (½ fl oz) Fig Syrup
- 30 ml (1 fl oz) fresh lemon juice
- 120 ml (4 fl oz) soda water (club soda)
- Fig half and rosemary sprig, to garnish

Fig Syrup

- 240 ml (8 fl oz) water
- 200 g (7 oz) granulated sugar
- 3–4 fresh figs, chopped
- 1 sprig fresh rosemary

METHOD

Make the sugar syrup. Bring the water to a boil in a saucepan, then add the sugar. Reduce to a simmer, stir until the sugar has dissolved, then add the figs.

Simmer for 15 minutes, crushing the figs to break them down. Add the rosemary and simmer for another 5 minutes.

Remove from the heat and allow to infuse for 30 minutes. Strain into a sealable container.

Add the vodka, fig syrup and lemon juice to a cocktail shaker with ice. Shake vigorously until cold, then strain into a rocks glass or tumbler filled with ice.

Top with the soda water, garnish and serve.

Earl Grey Tea Spritz

A twist on the spritz theme with a gentle note of bergamot from Earl Grey tea. For added botanicals, use gin instead of the vodka. The essential ingredients in a spritz are bitters and fizz, and the bitter orange note is found in both the bergamot and the Cointreau. Sweetened with honey and boosted by prosecco, this one is perfect for a special afternoon tea.

INGREDIENTS

- 1 tablespoon loose black Earl Grey tea, or 1 teabag
- 2 teaspoons honey
- 30 ml (1 fl oz) vodka
- 15 ml (½ fl oz) Cointreau
- 15 ml (½ fl oz) fresh lemon juice
- Chilled prosecco, to top
- Lemon slice, to garnish

METHOD

Steep the loose tea or teabag in 90 ml (3 fl oz) of boiling water for 10 minutes, then strain and stir in the honey until dissolved.

Pour the tea, vodka, Cointreau and lemon juice into a mixing glass and stir to combine.

Pour into a Kilner (Mason) jar or tumbler filled with ice. Top with the prosecco. Garnish with the lemon slice and serve.

VARIATION

Substitute a botanical dry gin, such as Hendrick's or Bombay Sapphire, for the vodka.

Serves 6–8

Apple Sangria

An autumnal version of the popular summertime Spanish sangria made with red wine, this is a fizzy apple drink accented by a hit of brandy. Use cloudy apple juice (apple cider) instead of clear apple juice as you want the drink to be tangy and not too sweet.

INGREDIENTS

- 350 ml (12 fl oz) cloudy apple juice (apple cider)
- 30 ml (1 fl oz) fresh lemon juice
- 60 ml (2 fl oz) fresh orange juice
- 50 ml (1½ fl oz) apple or apricot brandy
- 1 orange, sliced
- 1 green apple, diced
- 1 red apple, diced
- 8 thyme sprigs
- 3 cinnamon sticks
- 1 bottle chilled prosecco
- Extra thyme and cinnamon, to garnish

METHOD

Combine the apple, lemon and orange juices and the brandy in a large jug, stirring to combine.

Add in the fruit, thyme and cinnamon and leave to infuse in the refrigerator for 30 minutes. Just before serving, add in the prosecco and gently stir.

Serve in tumblers, making sure each glass includes apples and oranges, and garnish with thyme and cinnamon.

Serves 1

Cherry Smash

A pretty drink with an aromatic thyme garnish to add a herbal note to each sip. A 'smash' cocktail always includes fresh fruit, and here cherries make a welcome change from the more usual berries. Black cherries can be much sweeter than lighter-skinned varieties, so if you're using super-sweet ripe black cherries, use slightly less agave and check the balance before adding the prosecco.

INGREDIENTS

- 50 g (2 oz) fresh cherries, pitted
- 30 ml (1 fl oz) vodka
- 2 teaspoons fresh lemon juice
- 2 teaspoons agave syrup
- 150 ml (5 fl oz) chilled prosecco
- Thyme sprig and fresh cherries, to garnish

METHOD

Place your cherries in a blender and blitz until they are puréed. Fill a balloon glass with crushed ice and spoon over the purée.

Put the vodka, lemon juice and agave syrup in a cocktail shaker with ice and shake vigorously until cold. Pour into the glass over the cherry purée and stir.

Top with prosecco, garnish with the thyme and cherries, and serve.

CHERRIES

Depending on where you live, cherries are in season from spring to early autumn. Sweeter varieties are available earlier in the season, with tart versions appearing later. You can substitute defrosted frozen cherries for fresh in the recipe.

Blueberry Mimosa

Here is a wonderful way to use fresh blueberries gathered in late summer and autumn, depending on where you live. Just like when picking for preserves, choose plump, dark blue fruit that is easy to remove and has a nice flavour. The flavour is the most intense a few days after they turn deep blue.

INGREDIENTS

- 1 tablespoon Blueberry Syrup
- 60 ml (2 fl oz) flat lemonade
- Chilled prosecco, to top
- Fresh blueberries and a lavender sprig, to garnish

Blueberry Syrup

- 240 ml (8 fl oz) water
- 200 g (7 oz) granulated sugar
- 200 g (7 oz) blueberries
- Zest of 1 lemon

METHOD

Make the syrup. Add all the ingredients to a saucepan and bring to a boil. Reduce the heat and simmer for about 5 minutes until the blueberries have lost their shape. Remove from the heat, allow to cool and then strain into a sealable container.

Place a tablespoon of blueberry syrup at the bottom of a flute, then pour over the lemonade. Top with prosecco and garnish with the blueberries and lavender.

Dragonfruit Fizz

With a magenta colour and the flavour of kiwi and pear, dragonfruit (pitaya) is the fruit of the cactus plant. Although plentiful throughout the summer and autumn in the northern hemisphere, the fruit is generally available all year round. You can also use a ready-made dragonfruit purée, either fresh or frozen.

INGREDIENTS

- 6–8 mint leaves
- ½ lime, quartered
- 60 ml (2 fl oz) Dragonfruit Purée
- 50 ml (1½ oz) vodka
- 175 ml (6 fl oz) sparkling lemonade
- Mint sprigs and dragon fruit slice, to garnish

Dragonfruit Purée

- 1 pink-fleshed, ripe dragonfruit
- 1 tablespoon fresh lime juice
- ½ teaspoon agave syrup

METHOD

Make the purée. Cut the dragonfruit in half and scoop out the flesh and seeds. Place in a blender with the lime juice and agave syrup and blend until smooth. Extra purée can be stored in the fridge for 3 days.

Muddle the mint and lime in a cocktail shaker. Add the dragonfruit purée and vodka and shake with ice until cold.

Strain into a highball glass and top with the sparkling lemonade. Garnish and serve.

VARIATION

Add 60 ml (2 oz) of pineapple juice to make a tropical version for summertime drinking.

Pear Prosecco

Ginger syrup from a jar of stem ginger adds a warm, sweet and dessert-like flavour to a pear-flavoured gin cocktail. You can use any pears grown locally to you, but the best are ripe Anjou or Bartlett, which also work well in a homemade sugar syrup.

INGREDIENTS

- 60 ml (2 fl oz) pear juice or pear purée
- 60 ml (2 fl oz) gin
- 1 teaspoon stem ginger syrup
- ½ teaspoon fresh lemon juice
- Chilled sparkling wine of your choice, to top
- Pear slice and thyme sprig, to garnish

METHOD

Pour the pear juice, gin, stem ginger syrup and lemon juice into a cocktail shaker with ice. Shake vigorously, then strain into a chilled flute.

Top with the sparkling wine, garnish with the pear slice and thyme sprig, and serve.

VARIATION

Substitute vodka for the gin. A pear-flavoured vodka will give you a fruitier flavour.

Pumpkin Spice Spritz

If you love your seasonal pumpkin spice latte or slice of pumpkin pie, this cocktail is for you. Ideal for Halloween parties or bonfire nights, it is made with tinned pumpkin purée, though you can make your own by steaming and mashing peeled and deseeded pumpkin chunks.

INGREDIENTS

- 50 ml (1½ fl oz) whiskey
- 1 teaspoon maple syrup
- 30 ml (1 fl oz) pumpkin purée
- Sparkling clementine juice, or alternatively tangerine or orange
- Clementine slice and star anise, to garnish

For the rim

- Pumpkin spice mix
- Granulated sugar
- Lemon wedge

METHOD

To prepare the glass, mix the sugar and pumpkin spice in a saucer. Wet the rim of a balloon glass with the lemon, then dip into the mix. Chill in the refrigerator.

Combine the whiskey, maple syrup and pumpkin purée in a cocktail shaker with ice and shake vigorously until cold.

Strain into the prepared glass filled with ice, top with the sparkling juice and stir gently. Garnish with clementine and star anise, and serve.

PUMPKIN SPICE MIX

Pumpkin spice contains cinnamon, ginger, nutmeg, allspice and cloves, but you can substitute ground cinnamon for the rim.

WINTER

Warm up in winter with the smoky flavours of cognac and bourbon, enriched with the deep fruitiness of cranberry and raspberry, clementine and cherry. You'll find the traditional spice notes of cinnamon, nutmeg, clove and star anise, as well as green herbal rosemary, in the recipes in this chapter.

Celebrate the holiday season with champagne cocktails and festive drinks such as the glittery Vanilla Bourbon Fizz, the Nordic Sunrise, based on the caraway-flavoured aquavit, or the Snowball, a sparkling version of the advocaat Christmas drink. There are drinks for every social event – cozy at-home family gatherings, casual get-togethers with friends or formal and themed parties.

Manzanasada

The Manzanasada was created by mixologists Tad Carducci and Paul Tanguay. This version has the addition of apple brandy to give it an extra fruity flavour that makes a delicious drink for the colder months of the year.

INGREDIENTS

- 30 ml (1 fl oz) blanco tequila
- 15 ml (½ fl oz) mezcal
- 30 ml (1 fl oz) cloudy apple juice (apple cider)
- 25 ml (¾ fl oz) fresh lemon juice
- 15 ml (½ fl oz) apple brandy or calvados
- Ginger beer, to top
- Red apple slices, to garnish

METHOD

Pour the tequila, mezcal, apple juice, lemon juice and apple brandy into a cocktail shaker with ice. Shake vigorously until cold, then strain over ice into a highball glass.

Top up with ginger beer, stir and garnish with red apple slices.

MEZCAL AND TEQUILA

What is the difference? Tequila is made only with blue weber agave, whereas mezcal can be made from any type. While tequila has a bright and clean taste, mezcal is smokier in flavour due to the roasting method used in its production.

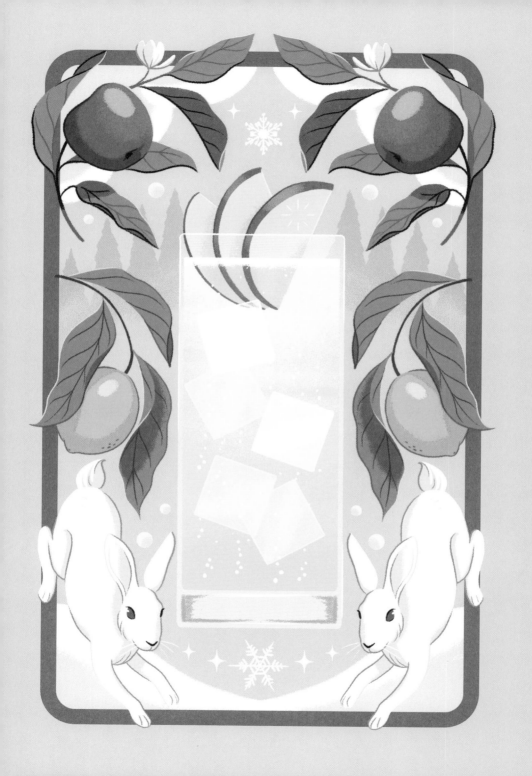

B&B Royale

A classic cocktail, the B&B is named for the ingredients brandy and Bénédictine, a French herbal liqueur said to have been developed by monks at a Benedictine Abbey in Normandy (hence the name). The cocktail delivers a complex honey taste that is sweetened and deepened with the addition of raspberry. This sparkling version delivers a lighter flavour that transitions the drink from an after-dinner offering to an aperitif.

INGREDIENTS

- 50 ml (1½ fl oz) cognac
- 25 ml (¾ fl oz) Bénédictine
- 15 ml (½ fl oz) black raspberry liqueur, such as Chambord
- Chilled champagne, to top
- Mint sprig and raspberry, to garnish

METHOD

Pour the cognac, Bénédictine and raspberry liqueur into a mixing glass with ice. Stir, then strain into a chilled coupe.

Top with champagne, garnish with the mint and raspberry, and serve.

BÉNÉDICTINE

The recipe for this herbal liqueur is a closely guarded secret. It is thought to contain a cornucopia of 27 herbs and spices, including juniper, myrrh, clove, honey, cinnamon, orange peel and vanilla.

El Diablo

This devilishly red drink appeared in a 1940s cocktail recipe book, *Trader Vic's Bartender's Guide*, as the Mexican Diablo. Trader Vic, founder of the eponymous chain of restaurants, was Victor Bergeron, who created the Mai Tai and popularized tiki culture. El Diablo is built straight into the glass so is fast to mix up – but with its tequila base and fiery ginger beer, this is a drink to sip slowly …

INGREDIENTS

- 30 ml (1 fl oz) tequila
- 30 ml (1 fl oz) crème de cassis
- Dash fresh lime juice
- 30 ml (1 fl oz) ginger beer
- Lime slice, to garnish

METHOD

Build this drink in the glass. Fill a highball three-quarters full with crushed ice, then pour in the tequila, crème de cassis and lime juice. Stir carefully to combine.

Top with the ginger beer, garnish with the lime and serve.

CRÈME DE CASSIS

The blackcurrant liqueur is a speciality from Burgundy in France and synonymous with the two-ingredient Kir (cassis with white wine) and Kir Royale (cassis with champagne). It is very sweet, and can be served as an after-dinner liqueur.

Champagne Cocktail

This classic cocktail, dating back to at least 1862 when it appeared (without the cognac) in *Jerry Thomas' Bar-Tenders Guide*, is perfect for the Christmas holidays. It is built right in the flute, so there's no need for a mixing glass. Traditionally served with champagne, you can also substitute any dry sparkling wine, such as cava or prosecco.

INGREDIENTS

- 1 white sugar cube
- 4 dashes Angostura bitters
- 30 ml (1 fl oz) cognac
- Chilled champagne
- Maraschino cherry, to garnish

METHOD

Soak the sugar cube in the Angostura bitters in a chilled champagne flute. Pour over the cognac and top with the champagne. Garnish with the maraschino cherry and serve.

VARIATION

Swap the Angostura bitters for Peychaud's, which is redder in colour and has notes of anise, cherry, clove, mint and orange.

Vanilla Bourbon Fizz

Edible gold gives this cocktail a touch of magic – ideal for the festive season – and the warm bourbon and vanilla notes make it a great choice for the winter months. You can buy edible gold as glitter, which you can stir in to add sparkle through the whole glass, or as flakes to sprinkle on top. For an indulgent version, upgrade to champagne in place of the prosecco. This is a recipe on the sweeter side and would be the perfect partner for a celebration cake.

INGREDIENTS

- 50 ml (1½ fl oz) bourbon
- Dash vanilla syrup or a drop of vanilla extract
- 15 ml (½ fl oz) sugar syrup (see page 11)
- Chilled prosecco, to top
- Star anise and gold edible glitter, to garnish

METHOD

Place the bourbon, vanilla and sugar syrup in a cocktail shaker with ice and shake vigorously until cold.

Strain into a chilled flute, top with prosecco and garnish with star anise and the edible glitter.

EDIBLE GLITTER

Glitter will settle in the drink so tap it over the top of the cocktail just before serving. If necessary, give the cocktail a gentle stir or tip it slightly to get the glitter moving. You can also add glitter to ice cubes or brush garnishes with glitter.

Serves 1

The Hedgerow

This cocktail takes its name from the source of two of the main elements, sloe gin and cherry brandy – for top marks, use homemade sloe gin. The colour and warming sloe and cherry flavours make this a good one for the festive season, too. Add each ingredient carefully to achieve the layered effect, with the deep scarlet colour at the bottom of the glass.

INGREDIENTS

- 2 rosemary sprigs
- 50 ml (1½ fl oz) chilled prosecco
- 30 ml (1 fl oz) sloe gin
- 30 ml (1 fl oz) cherry brandy

METHOD

Bruise 1 rosemary sprig to release the essential oils and drop it into a coupe glass filled with crushed ice. Slowly pour over the prosecco. Then carefully pour in the sloe gin and cherry brandy, one by one, so that they sink to the bottom.

Garnish with the other rosemary sprig and serve.

VARIATION

Substitute blackberry liqueur (crème de mûre) for the cherry brandy and add fresh blackberries for a garnish instead of the rosemary.

Nordic Sunrise

Traditionally served as a neat shot or in tulip-shaped glasses during the Christmas holidays in Scandinavia, aquavit has an assertive flavour and it is the essential ingredient in the Nordic Sunrise. Because it is botanical and herbaceous, you can try it as a substitute for gin. It also pairs well with Aperol and lime for a midsummer drink.

INGREDIENTS

- 30 ml (1 fl oz) aquavit
- 50 ml (1½ fl oz) fresh grapefruit juice
- 1 teaspoon sugar syrup (see page 11)
- Chilled prosecco, to top
- Grapefruit twist, to garnish

METHOD

Pour the aquavit, grapefruit juice, and sugar syrup into a cocktail shaker with ice. Shake vigorously until cold.

Strain into a chilled coupe and top with the prosecco. Garnish with a grapefruit twist.

AQUAVIT

Produced since the fifteenth century, the golden-coloured aquavit is a herbaceous Scandinavian spirit made from grain or potatoes and flavoured with botanicals, predominantly caraway. The Finnish version has a cinnamon flavour profile.

Negroni Sbagliato

Although Negroni Sbagliatos have been around for a few decades, they saw a resurgence in recent years thanks to a viral TikTok video. When asked for her favourite drink on a press tour for *House of the Dragon*, Emma D'Arcy delivered the iconic line: 'Negroni ... sbagliato ... with prosecco in it.' And its newfound audience love it for a reason: it's bittersweet, fruity, easy to assemble and a necessary addition to any cocktail collection.

INGREDIENTS

- 25 ml (¾ fl oz) sweet vermouth
- 25 ml (¾ fl oz) Campari
- 25 ml (¾ fl oz) prosecco
- Orange slice, to garnish

METHOD

Fill a mixing glass with ice. Add the vermouth and Campari. Stir until both liquids are thoroughly combined and chilled, then strain into a rocks glass.

Top with prosecco and stir gently again. Garnish with an orange slice and serve.

CAMPARI

Bitter, spicy and sweet, the distinctive red-coloured Campari was invented in 1860 by Gaspare Campari in Italy as an aperitivo. Often compared to Aperol, which is lighter in colour and sweeter, it has a deeper, more astringent flavour.

Serves 1

Sparking Snowball

A creamy retro drink for the winter festive season, the Snowball was thought to originate in 1940s England but became popular in the 1970s. The brandy is essential to cut through the sweetness of the advocaat (an egg yolk-based Dutch liqueur) but a dry sherry works well too.

INGREDIENTS

- 60 ml (2 fl oz) advocaat
- 30 ml (1 fl oz) brandy
- 15 ml (½ fl oz) lime cordial, such as Rose's
- 60 ml (2 fl oz) champagne or prosecco
- Maraschino cherry, to garnish

METHOD

Pour the advocaat, brandy and lime cordial into a cocktail mixer with ice and shake vigorously until cold.

Fill a highball with the champagne or prosecco and top with the strained advocaat mixture.

Stir gently, garnish with a maraschino cherry and serve.

VARIATION

Make a Russian Snowball by substituting a lemon-flavoured vodka for the brandy.

Christmas Cosmo

The holidays wouldn't be the same without cranberries in one form or another. Here we take the well-loved Cosmopolitan and create a less alcoholic sparkling version.

INGREDIENTS

- 4 fresh cranberries
- 50 ml (1½ fl oz) vodka
- 30 ml (1 fl oz) Cointreau
- 30 ml (1 fl oz) cranberry juice
- 15 ml (½ fl oz) fresh orange juice
- Sparkling apple juice, to top
- Rosemary sprig and cranberries, to garnish

METHOD

Muddle the cranberries in the bottom of a cocktail shaker. Add the vodka, Cointreau, cranberry juice and orange juice. Shake with ice until very cold. Double strain into a balloon glass filled with ice.

Top with the sparkling apple juice, garnish with the rosemary and cranberries, and serve.

VARIATION

Make a London Christmas Cosmo by using dry gin instead of vodka; omit the orange juice and use sparkling wine for the apple juice.

Sparkling Last Word

The Last Word cocktail – equal parts gin, chartreuse, maraschino syrup and fresh lime – is a Prohibition-era drink that was revived in the early 2000s by Seattle bartender Murray Stenson. This one, heavier on the gin and chartreuse, is herbaceous and fizzy with notes of pine, mint and citrus.

INGREDIENTS

- 50 ml (1½ fl oz) green Chartreuse
- 50 ml (1½ fl oz) gin
- 30 ml (1 fl oz) maraschino syrup (liqueur)
- 30 ml (1 fl oz) fresh lime juice
- Sparkling wine of your choice, to top
- Maraschino cherry, to garnish

METHOD

Pour the green Chartreuse, gin, maraschino syrup and lime juice in a cocktail shaker with ice and shake vigorously until very cold.

Strain into a chilled flute. Top with the sparkling wine, garnish with a cherry and serve.

VARIATION

To make a classic Last Word, omit the sparkling wine and increase the maraschino syrup and lime juice to 50 ml (1½ fl oz) each.

Serves 1

Mulled Wine Sparkler

A variation on the warm winter favourite, this bubbly mulled wine, served cold, has all the deep rich flavour of the original hot drink but with an effervescent finish.

INGREDIENTS

- 50 ml (1½ fl oz) spiced rum
- 15 ml (½ fl oz) port
- 30 ml (1 fl oz) Spiced Syrup
- 20 ml (⅔ fl oz) fresh clementine juice
- Sparkling wine, to top
- Orange twist, to garnish

Spiced Syrup

- 240 ml (8 fl oz) water
- 200 g (7 oz) granulated sugar
- 1 cinnamon stick
- ½ nutmeg, grated
- 2 cloves
- 1 vanilla pod (bean), split

METHOD

Make the syrup. Put the water, sugar, cinnamon, nutmeg, cloves and vanilla in a saucepan and bring to a boil. Reduce the heat and simmer for 15 minutes, stirring, until the sugar has dissolved. Set aside to cool. Then strain the liquid and pour into a clean sealable container.

Pour the rum, port, spiced syrup and clementine juice into a cocktail shaker filled with ice and shake vigorously until very cold.

Strain into a rocks glass with ice, top up with the sparkling wine and stir gently. Garnish with the orange twist and serve.

Valentine Love Bomb

With the emphasis on roses and pomegranate (in the grenadine and juice), this Valentine's Day treat is perfect for the most romantic time of the year. The pomegranate is associated with Aphrodite, the Greek goddess of love, marriage and fertility.

INGREDIENTS

- 60 ml (2 fl oz) gin
- 30 ml (1 fl oz) grenadine
- 15 ml (½ fl oz) pomegranate juice
- 1 teaspoon rosewater
- 3 frozen raspberries
- Chilled champagne or prosecco, to top
- Edible rose petals, to garnish

METHOD

Place the gin, grenadine, pomegranate juice and rosewater in a cocktail shaker with ice and shake vigorously for 30 seconds until cold.

Place the raspberries at the bottom of a chilled martini glass and strain the cocktail mixture into the glass.

Top with the champagne, garnish with the rose petals and serve.

ROSEWATER

Frequently used in beauty treatments and desserts such as Turkish delight, rosewater is made by steeping rose petals in water. Non-alcoholic, it has a delicate, sweet, floral taste that enhances the flavour of berries in cocktails.

Index

Acknowledgements

The publishers would like to thank Julia Murray for her evocative and beautiful illustrations. To see more of her work, see www.jumurray.com.

Thanks also go to Lucy Palmer for her graphic design and Theresa Bebbington for contributing the introductory text to this book.